from these

BROKEN
PIECES

true stories of redemption

Katie Hauck Ministries

CONTENTS

To the broken person reading this,
it isn't too late.
And for the one praying
over a shattered friend,
don't give up.

HI, I'M KATIE

I'm not a stranger to broken pieces. I got married at eighteen. I imagined growing old with my high school sweetheart, but eight years later I found myself a single mom with two little boys. I was shattered. I had no idea what to do next or how to put my life back together.

What I learned is that I *couldn't*. Not on my own. No matter what I did, I wasn't strong enough, good enough, or *anything* enough to heal what had been torn apart.

But God could and He did.

I began seeking Him and reading His Word. I started attending church and learned about my Savior. God crossed my path with an amazing man who would later become my husband. My family grew to be a home full of love. God took what was broken and He turned it into a work of art.

My story isn't unique. Healing, restoration, and redemption is what Jesus does. Over the past several months, I have had the honor of interviewing some incredible people who have had their lives radically transformed by God's love. What started as a You-

Tube series has been transcribed and adapted by my team at Katie Hauck Ministries to be the book now in your hands.

Get ready to read about real people who were torn apart by addiction and put back together by Jesus. Watch parents get reunited with their children and children be reunited with their parents. Witness the power of a praying mom and the unrelenting love of God. Make sure you have a Bible close because at the end of every chapter there will be Bible references and questions to help you go deeper.

Whether you are someone still trying to put your life back together or a long-time believer, I pray you are encouraged, inspired, and challenged by the stories you are about to read.

Friend, you are so incredibly loved by your heavenly Father and He has an incredible plan for your life. *Nothing* is too broken for Him to fix, but don't just take my word for it.

Let these stories show you.

3 DAYS

A jolt shook Lacy's stomach as the child growing inside her fought for life. Lacy's hand shook as she made the mark on the chart. It was only the eighth movement that hour. She pinched her eyes shut. First, she'd cried. Panicked. Now, she was beyond that. She was desperate, and the worst thing was that it was her fault.

She traced a finger over the scars on her arm. Drug scars, drugs that were now trying to stop her baby's heart.

"God," she sobbed. There was no one else she could call on. The doctors said it was just a matter of time before her baby died inside her.

Her baby.

Her fault.

No. Please.

She ran a hand over her bulging stomach and prayed. The words jumbled together as tears poured down her cheeks. "God, please. *Please*. Heal my body. Heal my daughter."

A day passed. Nothing

Another day. No change.

Another.

In a daze, she returned to the doctor. She knew the routine by now. Stress test. Vitals. Prayer, lots of desperate prayer.

"Hmm," the nurse said, checking a chart.

"What?" Lacy asked, fear shooting through her. Would today be when she got the devastating news?

The nurse said nothing and left the room. Lacy's world spun as she waited, and her panic erupted as the door opened. The nurse returned with the doctor.

This was it. The thought landed with a thud in her stomach.

The doctor ran a hand across his chin. "I'm not really sure what happened."

"What?" Lacy's voice quivered.

"The vitals are good. Heart rate levels are normal." The doctor raised his gaze to meet her eyes. "Your body healed itself. Your baby is healthy."

And Lacy collapsed. "It was God. It has to be Him."

Jesus kind of has this habit of changing everything in just three days.[1]

Lacy has been the program director of one of the women's rehabilitation homes at True Purpose Ministries for about five years. She's no longer the woman who couldn't operate without drugs. She's no longer a thief and a liar. No longer is her home a couch or a car. No longer is her life a mess of destruction, chaos,

---

[1]   Jesus was crucified and buried, but the grave could not hold Him! Three days later, He was alive again. This moment completely transformed history and is the corner-stone of the Christian faith. Learn more about this event by reading Matthew 28, Mark 16, Luke 24, or John 20.

and brokenness. Instead, she built a life for herself and her healthy, wonderful daughter.

There is nothing too broken for the Lord to heal.

Piece It Together

Read Luke 8:43-48.

God's miraculous healings were recorded in scripture, but we know He still heals today. Is this difficult for you to accept? Why or why not?

_____

_____

_____

What are you dealing with that needs to be healed? This could be physically, spiritually, or emotionally.

_____

_____

_____

_____

Write your favorite Bible verse about God's healing power and then speak it out loud.

_____

_____

_____

_____

Take a moment now to pray and ask God for the healing you need. Record anything He reveals to you during this time.

_____

_____

_____

_____

FREEDOM

Prison. Carlos stared at the front of the courtroom with a pit in his stomach. The judge rattled off the charges. Five years for this, five years for that. Add another six months. The time Carlos would be behind bars built up to a weight that threatened to crush him.

Carlos swallowed. "Your honor, I'm no mathematician, but that's eleven years."

The judge tapped his paperwork. "Yes, it is, Mr. Garcia. Nice to know there is something in that head of yours."

His stomach plummeted. This was real. No more running. No more getting away with his crimes. In a daze, he was led back to the bullpen. Concrete walls surrounded Carlos, choking him. Carlos struggled to breathe as the judge's words sank in.

He collapsed into a chair, fingers drumming on his leg. His mom had warned him. So. Many. Times. "Change your circle of friends," she'd said. "Look at the people you hang out with, Carlos." She'd given him warning after warning, and yet he'd ignored her. Now, it was too late. He was trapped.

Carlos sucked in a shaky breath and whispered, "God, You have my undivided, full attention."

Moments later, the door opened and his attorney walked in. Her eyes pierced straight through him as she slid into the chair across from him.

"I'm guilty," Carlos murmured. No more excuses. He met the woman's gaze. "You know what, whatever it is, I'll go through it. I really don't want to go to prison, but I'm done with the games. I don't want—"

She held up her hand. "Mr. Garcia, forgive me for saying this, but do you know you have a call on your life?"

It was the last thing he'd expected her to ask. That one question broke something in Carlos. His throat closed off. He'd been running for so long. "Please help me," he pleaded.

She watched the tears run down his cheek for a minute. "Okay, lock it up and stop crying."

He cleared his throat. "Yes, ma'am."

"Do you trust me?" she asked.

Carlos didn't know this lady. This stranger. But there was something about her eyes. They didn't hold judgment; they didn't hold blame. All Carlos saw was love. A second chance.

"Sure."

The rest of the court appearance was a blur as the attorney got to work. Sixty days later, he walked out of jail with his time fully served. He could have—should have—gotten eleven years, but two months later he stepped out of his prison cell and into a world of freedom.

As it turned out, there was a call on his life. He now serves in full-time ministry.

Piece It Together

Read Acts 16:25-34.

Like Carlos, the Lord gave Paul and Silas physical freedom. They used this to bring others spiritual freedom. How can your story be used to help others find freedom in Christ?

_____

_____

_____

_____

Are you living in freedom? If not, how can you?

_____

_____

_____

_____

Write your favorite Bible verse about finding freedom through Christ and then speak it out loud.

_____

_____

_____

_____

Take a moment now to pray and ask God how He can use you to change lives. Record anything He reveals to you during this time.

_____

_____

_____

_____

THE GIFT

Lights twinkled and Christmas music played softly in the background as Tracy folded the wrapping paper around the box in front of her. A sweet aroma of peppermint and ginger hung in the air. It was surreal. Forty-two years ago, a Christmas like this would have been impossible. Her daughter—of all people!—was sitting beside her.

Tracy could still see her children's faces as she walked away from them all those years ago. Drugs had shut her body down, and years of silence stretched between her and her kids. Grandchildren came into the world, but her son said, "If you don't get your act together and get your life right, you will never know this baby. I will never let you meet her. I will never let you put your darkness into her." There was no room for debate.

Even Tracy's dad hated her. She went through life with glares, silence, and arguments.

Forty-two years of addiction. Forty-two years of pain. Forty-two years of tearing her family apart. She had lived for the high but had crushed her whole family when she dragged them down.

Now, here she was. Right beside her daughter.

Tracy glanced over at her and paused. It wasn't just Christmas lights reflecting in her daughter's eyes; no, those were tears.

"What's wrong?" Tracy asked.

"Mom," her daughter swiped at her eyes. "I waited all my life for the woman that's sitting right here on this couch with me."

Tracy pulled her daughter into a hug. "Lord, thank You," she whispered.

They wept together. Time lost all meaning as the hurt and pain of decades poured out and healed. They may have been wrapping Christmas gifts for others, but Tracy knew she'd gotten the greatest gift of all.

———————————

At fifty-four, Tracy is now a house director for True Purpose Ministries. She's a redeemed child of the Most High. Her life is teaching, speaking, and challenging women to grow closer to Jesus. She has even met her granddaughter.

"Never give up," she says. "The Lord goes after us, pursuing us constantly to bring us back home to Him. My salvation is the greatest gift I've ever received in any aspect of my life.

"So, grab a Bible, grab a friend, sit down, and open the book and read it together. Pray about what it is you want the Lord to tell you and trust that He's going to do just that. People, just keep going. You're not going to get it at first but keep going. Keep pressing forward. It's not meant to be easy, but it's worth it."

Piece It Together

Read Ephesians 2:8-9.

How has the gift of salvation changed your life?

_____

_____

_____

_____

Who is someone you need to reconcile with and what steps can you take to begin that process?

_____

_____

_____

_____

Write your favorite Bible verse about reconciliation and then speak it out loud.

_____

_____

_____

_____

Take a moment now to pray and ask God to bring reconciliation to your relationship. Record anything He reveals to you during this time.

_____

_____

_____

AND THERE
I MET JESUS

Eric had been dragged to church before. What would it hurt to go to church again now? He'd already ruined his life, after all. It wasn't like church could make it *worse*.

Drugs had gotten him here. He'd been in and out of jail since he was sixteen. All of his relationships were torn apart. There was nowhere for him to go.

So, somehow, he found himself in that church. He sat there and, with nothing better to do, listened to the pastor. The preacher's gaze bore straight into Eric's soul, and his words peeled back Eric's defenses. Something in Eric stirred that he didn't even know existed.

Eric couldn't get to that altar fast enough. He launched himself from his seat and tore to the front of the church. He threw himself to his knees, and right then and there met Jesus.

He still had growing to do. True Purpose and Celebrate Recovery helped him foster that relationship. Drugs, alcohol, and destruction were traded for peace, happiness, joy, and love.

"The love of God inside of me is just overflowing, and I want to give it to everyone so they can experience true love," he said. "We go through struggles, trials, and tribulations, but we often look in the wrong places for answers. Instead, we should turn to Jesus, who will help us along the way. No matter the difficulties, Jesus is right there with you, so never give up. Look up and keep pushing. Stay strong and look to God for all the answers."

Piece It Together

Read Luke 5:1-11.

What did you give up to follow Jesus?

_____

_____

_____

_____

What do you still struggle to give up?

_____

_____

_____

_____

Write your favorite Bible verse about how the Lord is our helper and then speak it out loud.

_____

_____

_____

_____

Take a moment now to pray and ask God to help you give up anything that interferes with you knowing Him. Record anything He reveals to you during this time.

_____

_____

_____

_____

KIDNAPPED TO FIND THE LIGHT

"Come on, Ryan. I'll take you to the store," Ryan's mother said as he stumbled into the car. The world was a fuzzed blur of color and light as he fumbled for the seat buckle.

His mother glanced back at him. "This is for your good," she murmured and shifted the car into drive.

Of course it was, Ryan thought. He needed to make this run to the store and he wasn't stupid, after all. He knew he wasn't in a condition to drive.

When it was just alcohol creeping into his life, he could pretend he had everything under control. He'd gone to work every day, made a good living, owned a house. He'd even had a motorcycle. On the outside, he'd looked like he had everything together.

But then the addiction sunk in deep. Depression set in. While his world was already unraveling, he found methamphetamine.

Ryan rested his head against the car window and watched as the streetlights and road signs zipped past. "Wait." He fought to straighten out his thoughts. "You missed the turn."

His mother pressed her lips into a thin line. "No, Ryan. I didn't. We're just taking a detour."

A detour? No. They had driven too far for this to be a different route. It had to be more than that.

This was a kidnapping.

"Stop!" he yelled, but his mom didn't listen. He dug out his phone and dialed 911. "Help, I'm being kidnapped!"

"What's going on?" Concern filled the dispatcher's voice.

"Tell her who's doing it," Ryan's mom ordered.

Ryan gripped the phone tighter. "My mom. My mom is kidnapping me. She was supposed to take me to the store, but she passed it and won't stop."

"Sir," the dispatcher's tone shifted, "call back if you are in danger."

The call ended and Ryan sank back against the seat. Time ran together as they drove. Maybe it was hours, maybe minutes, but eventually the car parked in front of a building with a sign saying True Purpose Ministries. Ryan threw off his seat belt and stormed out of the car.

A man intercepted him. "My name's Gage and we want to help you. Can we talk about this?" He led Ryan and his mom over to a picnic table. "Look, man, we're going to help you."

Ryan's mom let out a relieved sigh, but Gage wasn't finished. "But we don't have a bed available yet. If you can be back here in a week, we can let you into the program. Just give me a call by Friday."

Ryan nodded slowly. "OK."

His mom took him back to his girlfriend's house, but staying clean for a week was too much to ask. Within an hour, he was arrested.

"You get your one phone call," the police told him and Ryan called his mom.

"I'll bail you out," she said. "But you're staying with me until you're in True Purpose."

"Alright," Ryan said. "Whatever."

The jail time allowed Ryan to sober up and dry out. By the time he got to True Purpose, he was looking forward to rehab. This was his chance, and he was going to take it. From the moment he showed up at their doorstep, he knew he was supposed to be there. He didn't know the Jesus guy they talked about, but he was going to give Him a shot.

Now, Ryan is different. New. He's training to work on airplanes, beginning a two-and-a-half-year apprenticeship to get his aircraft license. He's going to learn to fly.

All because his mother wasn't willing to give up. Instead, she was willing to do whatever was necessary to help her son.

Piece It Together

Read Mark 2:2-5.

Sometimes we need some help getting to Jesus. Who brought you to Jesus?

_____

_____

_____

_____

Have you ever brought a friend to Jesus? How did your friend react?

_____

_____

_____

_____

Write your favorite Bible verse about sharing the gospel of Jesus Christ and then speak it out loud.

_____

_____

_____

_____

Take a moment now to pray and ask God if there is anyone in your life you need to share Jesus with. Record anything He reveals to you during this time.

_____

_____

_____

_____

DARE TO BELIEVE

The last thing Page wanted to do was walk through the door of The House That Mercy Built. Then again, she didn't have much of a choice. She could still hear the gavel bang as she was sentenced to serve out her court-ordered, year-long program to detox from drugs.

Her jaw was locked, her shoulders tensed. She did not want to be here. But where else could she go? Jail? Back to the streets?

She had no plans. No purpose. No goals. No hope. She'd never known someone who didn't do drugs. It was her past, her present, and undoubtedly her future. What insane person thought that showing up at this place would make any difference?

But then something strange happened.

She started meeting the other women. They were… different. They did things. Real things. Instead of wasting away on drugs, graduates of the program were going to school. They had careers. They had lives. They told stories of how the Lord had made that possible.

Yeah, Page heard a lot about this Lord. At first, her anger

burned too much to listen, but the words and the stories started to chip away at her rage until one day a thought flitted through her mind.

Maybe this could be for me.

She prayed to the Lord, "God, if You want this for me, I want it, too. I'm willing to yield to You, surrender to You. I'll allow You to teach me to have a different life. A better life." Page dared to believe.

It terrified her. People had let her down before, more times than she could count. Still, she couldn't do this halfway. No, she'd take the risk. It was time to go all in and see what happened.

Page's life transformed.

"God has fulfilled and gone beyond every promise I could ever have thought to ask. He has answered prayers I didn't even think to pray. He has connected dots, placed me with the right people, and allowed me to fulfill my calling."

She now serves as an executive director at True Purpose Ministries.

"He has done amazing things through my obedience," Page says. "God can do so much with one little 'yes' and a surrendered heart. Do not be afraid of change, and don't be afraid to get uncomfortable. You may have to endure withdrawal or face difficult challenges, but on the other side of that is a brand new life of freedom."

Piece It Together

Read Romans 8:28-30.

How has the decision to surrender to God changed your path in life?

_____

_____

_____

_____

Describe a time when God took a bad situation and used it for your good.

_____

_____

_____

_____

Write your favorite Bible verse about surrendering to God and then speak it out loud.

_____

_____

_____

_____

Take a moment now to pray and ask God to help you surrender daily to His will for your life. Record anything He reveals to you during this time.

_____

_____

_____

_____

.

THE DRINKING GAME

Kim leaned back in her kitchen chair and took another swig of her beer. Her friend mirrored her.

Kim bit her lip to keep from bursting out with laughter. They were a mess. Her second husband was in rehab for the thirteenth time. He was addicted; she was addicted. Drugs flowed through her blood. Her life was in shambles.

But somehow this woman across from her had it even worse.

Kim downed the rest of her drink and pointed at her friend. "Your life is a mess. You need to find Jesus."

Her friend's eyebrows arched. She set her drink down, a challenge glinting in her eyes. "Okay, let's go to church tomorrow."

Kim humphed. Sure. Whatever. She'd accept the challenge; she wouldn't back down.

Kim crawled out of bed the next morning with sluggish thoughts and a headache. Hungover, she stumbled into the church. Flashes of movement and noise whirled around her. It was strange. Different. Loud.

How long did this thing last?

They passed around a card asking for her name, number, and address. She filled it out. Maybe it was a raffle or something. This morning wouldn't be a total waste of time if she won a gift basket.

But sadly, the church didn't end the service with a drawing. She headed home, back to her drinks, her drugs, and her normal.

Monday night, the party was at her house. Football was on the TV as her home filled with other people looking for a break from reality. Kim kept a beer in one hand and a cigarette in the other.

A knock sounded on the door. Kim guessed her neighbors had decided to join the party. She sauntered over to the door and opened it wide.

It wasn't her neighbors.

Oh. My. God.

She recognized this man.

She'd seen him Sunday at that blasted church.

Kim's stomach twisted and suddenly she didn't feel all that buzzed. No, her thoughts were painfully clear. Something radiated off this man. God was with him. She could feel it. All Kim could do was stare at him as he looked back. A tremble filled her whole body and she tightened her grip on the door's threshold.

His face wore a small, reassuring smile. "I just wanted to tell you that we're so happy that you came to our church. If you ever need anything, come back." He turned around and left.

But the Holy Spirit stayed.

Kim's knees slammed against the floor as tears rolled down her cheeks. Time lost its meaning. It was dark. It was ugly. Suddenly, she could see her life for what it was. Kim could see the filth of her sin. She saw the reality of her life separated from God.

She was never meant to be that person.

A fire began to spread in her body, burning beneath her skin. Was this God's judgment, shoving her to Hell?

"God!" She choked out through her sobs. "If You'll help me, I'll follow You all the days of my life."

And God's love took over. An inferno of love melted away all that chained her and purified it.

Freedom.

She got off the floor. "I'll follow You. I'll go to the ends of the earth just to be near You, for whatever You want my life to be."

Everything changed. She didn't smoke, didn't drink, and her cravings evaporated. She was taken over by the love of God. She'd drive past the church and it didn't matter if it was Sunday or not, she'd be stopping in that building to praise the Lord.

Slowly, her life came back together. She divorced her constantly relapsing husband and grew closer to Jesus with her children. The Lord brought a godly man into her life. Together, they now do children's ministry all around the world.

Old friends still stop her. "What's the matter with you? This is going to wear off."

Kim just shakes her head and smiles. "Don't you see me? You saw me before. Don't you see me now?"

Kim is brand new.

Piece It Together

Read 2 Corinthians 5:17.

You can become a new creation, too. If you have never accepted Jesus Christ as your Lord and Savior, it's simple. Please consider saying these words out loud and believe them in your heart:

Heavenly Father, I believe with my heart and confess with my mouth that Jesus rose from the dead so that I can be saved. I ask You to come into my life and forgive me of my sin. I want to live to bring glory and honor to You. Thank You, Lord. Amen.

What does it mean to you to be a new creation in Christ?

_____

_____

_____

_____

What old things have passed away in your life and what has God replaced them with?

_____

_____

_____

_____

Write your favorite Bible verse about salvation and then speak it out loud.

_____

_____

_____

_____

Take a moment now to pray and thank God for what He's delivered you from. Record anything He reveals to you during this time.

_____

_____

_____

_____

CPR

This couldn't be happening. No. It had to just be a terrible nightmare.

Panic filled April as she stared down at her cousin. The room had cleared as soon as he started convulsing, and now she was desperately alone. Her cousin was overdosing on drugs and there was nothing she could do to stop it.

The thrashing stilled, and April choked back a sob. *He's dead*. The thought shook her to life, and she dove forward to pound on his chest. Her brain scrambled to remember the steps for CPR.

She puffed air into his lungs, begging him to take a breath. Finally, he gasped. Seventeen minutes later, he was back.

The tears hit April as her knees hit the ground. She'd already violated her Community Corrections; the Department of Children's Services was looking for her so they could take her child. She couldn't live like this anymore.

"God!" Desperation exploded inside her. "I can't do this. Please. You've got to come in and help me."

She choked on her sobs. Suddenly, she saw herself in her

cousin's shoes. What if she'd been the one who had stopped breathing? Her daughter would have been left alone. Motherless.

"I will take my daughter, Katie, and hand her over to DCS myself if that's what it's going to take for me to get somewhere and get clean," she prayed.

She had to change. *Had to*. She couldn't keep living like this. She couldn't keep pushing her hell onto her six-month-old child.

The phone rang mere hours later. "April?"

"I'm here."

"I've spoken with a woman at True Purpose Ministries, and they have a bed ready for you. You can bring your daughter."

Within four months, her DCS case closed, she was released from probation, and she had encounters with the Lord that would forever change her. Today, her marriage has been restored, and she has joined the staff at True Purpose Ministries. Plus, April and her husband are moving into their own home.

The CPR gave her cousin a second chance that night, but God did CPR on her, too. He brought her back to life. Restored her. Redeemed her.

She was never meant to be a drug addict; she was meant to be a child of God.

Piece It Together

Read Jonah 2:1-10.

Is there an area in your life where you'd like a second chance?

_____

_____

_____

_____

How would you do it differently this time?

_____

_____

_____

Write your favorite Bible verse about God's grace and then speak it out loud.

_____

_____

_____

_____

Take a moment now to pray and ask God to give you a second chance. Record anything He reveals to you during this time.

_____

_____

_____

_____

_____

_____

SOMETHING FOR ME

Peyton's eyes flew open. He was alive. Somehow, someway he had survived yet another overdose. That made five times. His first thought was, "Wow, so I know God has something for me." Only by a higher power could he have survived so many close calls with death.

Yeah, God had to be real, and there had to be a reason Peyton was alive, but he wasn't ready to do anything about that yet. Peyton had been high pretty much 24/7 from the time he was sixteen until now at twenty-two. He didn't know how to stop.

His mom was stuck on drugs, too. They'd had a falling out, but Peyton was ready to reconcile. Maybe that would be a good step in the right direction.

But when the phone rang, it brought a different message. "Peyton, your mother is dead." Fluid had built up in her lungs. She was gone.

The news slammed into him. That was it. No more. He went to

a clinic, desperate for help. They just got him addicted to some-thing else.

He was locked in this cycle of addiction, but then he found True Purpose Ministries and they took him in. They showed him Jesus. Only three and half months later, he started looking at going to barber school. He started writing and singing about Jesus in his rap music.

He came to True Purpose Ministries at a point when he didn't care if he died from drugs because he felt so alone. He knew he wasn't living right but also knew he could never fix it.

Good thing he didn't have to. Jesus stepped in and changed everything.

Piece It Together

Read Mark 2:17.

Jesus is looking for the people who are low and homeless, drug addicted and imprisoned. He's looking for the people living in misery. He's looking for you. How does that make you feel?

_____

_____

_____

_____

You are never alone. Describe a time you felt God's presence.

_____

_____

_____

_____

Write your favorite Bible verse that reminds you that you are not alone and then speak it out loud.

_____

_____

_____

_____

Take a moment now to pray and just sit in God's presence. Record anything He reveals to you during this time.

_____

_____

_____

_____

ARRESTED BY PRAYER

"Mom, I overdosed." Rebecca's hand shook as she clutched the phone to her ear.

Her life was chaos. Her children were separated from her—her daughter with her dad, and her son with the state. Her current address was under whatever bridge she could find. If she couldn't find a bridge, she'd just be on the streets. She never knew where her next meal would come from.

Rebecca also didn't know that on the other side of the phone, her mom was praying, "Lord, have my daughter arrested. Better a jail cell, than dead."

It only took a couple of days for that prayer to be answered. Rebecca found an unlikely safe place behind bars.

A month later, her sister told her the story. "After you told us that you overdosed, mom took it to the altar and prayed for you to get arrested." God had stepped in.

Rebecca didn't know who this God was, but if He was able to

get her off the streets and into the safety of a jail cell, she wanted to meet Him.

"I need a Bible," she thought. "I need to find out what this is."

For the first time in her life, she opened God's Word. Her fingers thumbed through the thin pages. Where did she start with this? Who was this Jesus guy?

She was released to True Purpose Ministries, and it was there she found Him. She was saved, brought out of the darkness, and for the first time that she could remember, she felt alive.

Truly alive.

She thought she was worthless; she discovered she was loved. She thought life was hopeless; she discovered her story wasn't finished yet.

A prayer may have put her in prison, but it also paved the way to find true freedom.

Piece It Together

Read 1 Samuel 1:10-20.

Describe a time in your life you prayed desperately for something and God answered.

_____

_____

_____

_____

What is something you are still praying for?

_____

_____

_____

_____

Write your favorite Bible verse about prayer and then speak it out loud.

_____

_____

_____

_____

Take a moment now to pray and thank God for hearing your prayers. Record anything He reveals to you during this time.

_____

_____

_____

_____

WHO AM I?

Who am I?

The question spun in Nate's mind. He'd grown up in Taylor, Virginia, so maybe that meant he was a Virginian. He'd been playing sports since fifth grade, so maybe he was an athlete. He enjoyed fishing, hunting, and shooting guns, so maybe he was an outdoorsman. But either way, he didn't feel like he belonged anywhere.

Not really.

What was wrong with him? He couldn't quite make the friends he wanted. He was the best field goal kicker on the football team—people appreciated his talent—but he could tell their attention never went so deep as to appreciate *him*.

And then, suddenly, he found his way in.

Drugs. Alcohol. He sold it to the other football team guys while he experimented with it himself. They accepted him then, even welcomed him. They called his name from across the hall of the school. Slapped him on the back like one of the pack.

He got a scholarship to go to Carson-Newman to keep playing

football. It could have been the opportunity of a lifetime, but he carried his addiction with him. As drugs tanked his academics and his football performance dwindled, his scholarship evaporated.

Now what?

He couldn't be accepted at college. Couldn't be accepted at home. The devastation broke through his last remaining boundaries and the next time he came across harder drugs, he used them.

It was too much for his body to take. He overdosed once.

Twice.

Three times.

Four.

He got second chances. He was back on the football team. He was once again benched on the football team. He tried drug programs. They'd straighten him out for a while, but nothing would last. An officer allowed him to return home for Christmas and then turn himself in, but Nate couldn't stay clean at home. His second chances turned into more drugs and more overdosing.

There wasn't a single place he felt accepted. Not college. Not the football team. Not home.

Who am I?

Who am I?

Who. Am. I?

Or maybe the better question was, how far was too far before he was nothing but a drug addict?

His coach was friends with a pastor who knew about this faith-based organization dedicated to lasting recovery. Nate begrudgingly gave it a chance and was amazed.

All those Christians *welcomed* him in. Accepted him. Loved

him. Challenged him to be better. Jesus looked at Nate and didn't just see the drug addict. Didn't just see the football player. No, He saw so much more.

Who am I?

Nate is a child of God.

Piece It Together

Nate was so desperate for acceptance that he looked for it in all the wrong places. Truly, what he was looking for was unconditional love, and that is found only in Jesus.

Read John 15:12-17.

How does it make you feel that Jesus doesn't just want to be your savior but also your friend?

_____

_____

_____

What does this passage tell you about your identity?

_____

_____

_____

_____

Write your favorite Bible verse about who you are in Christ and then speak it out loud.

_____

_____

_____

Take a moment now to pray and thank God for His friendship. Record anything He reveals to you during this time.

_____

_____

_____

_____

ONE MORE CHANCE

Please let me come back. Anjeliah pushed send on the text to True Purpose Ministries. *Please, I have no other option.*

Anjeliah had been to this faith-based drug rehab program before, but she couldn't keep her head on straight and was kicked out after three weeks. They let her come back but after a few months, drama with the other girls and a relapse after cheating the system got her kicked out again.

But in the back of her mind, she saw a future with recovery. She just hadn't been ready before, that was all. Now, she was desperate. Now, she had children depending on her. Her twelve-year-old son had watched her overdose. She couldn't let that happen again.

She kept sending texts.

Please.

Please.

Then, a text came through with a soft ping.

Come by next week and you can come back into the program.

Anjeliah's heart skipped a beat. Here was chance number

three. This time, she was determined for it to work, and she knew the only way it could. The first and second time she'd been at True Purpose Ministries she hadn't read her Bible. She'd still lied, still acted with her old flesh, and still gave into hypocrisy. It was time to let the Lord take over.

And He restored her life. She got a car and got a job. She was promoted to manager at a local fast-food restaurant. She became a house mom at the very program that accepted her back again. She has been clean for over eighteen months, which is the longest she's been clean since she started doing drugs at sixteen.

Sometimes you need more than a second chance. Sometimes it takes a third, or a fourth, or a fifth.

Don't. Give. Up.

Piece It Together

Read Mark 14:66-72.
Read John 21:15-25.

Peter majorly messed up here. He denied Jesus three times! But then Jesus gave him three chances to proclaim his love for the Lord. Don't let the number of times you've messed up stop you from coming back to Jesus. He'll just let the number of your mistakes be how many times you say "I love You" back.

Where in your life have you messed up?

_____

_____

_____

_____

_____

_____

_____

Think about what Jesus would say to you if you were standing face to face with Him today and write His loving words down.

_____

_____

_____

_____

_____

_____

_____

Write your favorite Bible verse about forgiveness and then speak it out loud.

_____

_____

_____

_____

Take a moment now to pray and thank the Lord for giving you so many chances. Record anything He reveals to you during this time.

_____

_____

_____

_____

A WALK THROUGH A STORM

Wind roared in Sean's ears. Rain pounded on his head, dripping down his hair and into his eyes. Lightning flashed in the distance, and a thunderclap echoed after it. The only clothes he owned were soaked through, but still he kept going.

Sean put one foot in front of the other. It was a slow process, but that wasn't anything new to Sean.

For half his life, he'd been addicted and in prison. He'd alienated most of the people he knew, and those he still had contact with were just as addicted to drugs as he was. Anger had burned inside of him.

But then one day he found a Bible and he began to read it, one verse at a time. Every day, he opened that Bible and read. God's Word penetrated the anger and hopelessness and started to build something new. They had tablets in prison where he could watch church services. Suddenly, scripture was pouring into his life. It wasn't easy—the anger and pain weren't over—and it wasn't overnight, but day by day, it got a little easier.

Then came the day that the prison bars rolled back, and he took his first steps into freedom. But where was he supposed to go? There was no family to take him in, no friends he cared to see again. Nothing. He had nothing.

But the words of the preachers he'd watched on that tablet echoed in his ears. "If you ever get out of that jail, come on down."

The storm was already raging outside, but that didn't matter to Sean. He took his first step from the prison and out into the rain. One step in front of the other, all the way to Rio Revolution Church.

He hesitated at the church's glass door. A puddle gathered around his feet.

A man opened the door wide. "Come on in. How can we help you?"

Sean fumbled through his story, how he'd been in prison and listened to the sermons that led him here. He waited for what the man would say. Maybe he would give Sean a place to stay for the night. Sean figured he'd be on the streets for a while, but one night to get his bearings would be amazing.

"Let me make a call," the man said and returned a few moments later. "We can get you into True Purpose Ministries. I'll drive you over."

Sean didn't know what True Purpose Ministries was, but anything was better than what he had. So, he followed the man out of the church and into a car to drive over. There, he found a place to sleep, a place to readjust to society, but most importantly, a place to grow closer to the Lord.

It was worth a walk in the rain.

Piece It Together

The changes that took place in Sean's life—the discovery of hope and the will to live—were due to his time spent in God's Word. He just opened it up and let the Lord work how He willed. It was slow progress, like his walk in the rain, but within only seven months, he'd already come to a place where he wanted to live again, where he had hope, where he felt loved.

If you don't read your Bible consistently, start today. Just open up God's Word and read a few verses each day.

If you are new to reading your Bible daily, I recommend starting with one of the Gospels: Matthew, Mark, Luke, or John. That way you can read about the amazing life of Jesus, our Lord and Savior. Psalms or Proverbs may be good options, too, if you want something shorter but still full of life-changing scripture.

Read 2 Timothy 3:16-17.

Where will you start reading the Bible today?

_____

_____

_____

_____

Write down a plan to incorporate reading the Bible into your schedule.

_____

_____

_____

_____

Write your favorite Bible verse about seeking God and then speak it out loud.

_____

_____

_____

_____

Take a moment now to pray and ask the Lord to show Himself to you through His Word. Record anything He reveals to you during this time.

_____

_____

_____

_____

LOVE STORY

She was gone. Stephen's baby girl was gone. Corrina had only been five weeks old when she'd passed away in his bed. How do you escape pain like that?

He reached for some methamphetamine and let it kill the pain, kill him. He didn't care anymore. Let the drugs do what they may. He was already walking down a slippery slope before he lost his child. By the time Stephen was five or six years old, his parents were already out of the picture. The revolving door of foster care was his reality. A few years passed and he found himself in detention centers. After that, it was prison for six years.

He didn't doubt there was a God; he'd experienced a miracle when he'd watched his little girl be born. He did doubt that this God was good.

"Who are you to take her away?!" he screamed.

His mind constantly replayed the day she'd died. He could still see the flashing lights of the ambulance in front of him. He could still see the room where he'd been questioned like a criminal. "You can't leave town until the autopsy," the detectives had said, like he was the one who had hurt his Corrina.

Pain was a beast inside of Stephen, tearing him apart. For fourteen years, he let drugs dull the world while he unraveled.

Then, somehow, he found himself sitting in a church. Why was he even doing this? They were just going to tell him how bad he was. "Turn or burn" and all of that. He didn't have to be told anything to know it was true. He was already living in hell, after all.

But the guy who got up on the platform that day had something different to say. He was preaching about a Man who died on the cross for Stephen's sins. He was preaching about a Man who loved and cared about him so much that He went through horrendous things so that people like Stephen wouldn't have to live in the hell he'd been living in. It caught Stephen's attention. He was curious.

Four years later, he found himself at True Purpose Ministries. The only clothes he owned bore his prison number, but they gave him a whole new wardrobe and offered him the bottom bunk. He didn't even have to fight for it. These people were different. They loved one another. They supported one another. They knew how to take the Word of God, mix it with the Holy Spirit and some godly wisdom, and feed young Christians like Stephen until he was able to open up a Bible of his own and start feeding himself.

Slowly, the drugs lost their appeal and Jesus stitched up the wounds in Stephen's heart.

He wasn't the man he used to be.

———————

Who was that guy? Catt tried her best to focus on the church service, but her thoughts kept flitting back to the man she'd spotted earlier. Clearly, he was right out of prison, bless him. He wore a white T-shirt and knee-high socks. All that was missing was his prison number. Still, there was something about him that just seemed special.

She refocused on the worship service, a smile on her face.

God was so, so good. She'd grown up in church, but it had been a work-based faith. Her family hid its abuse. She'd carried struggles with self-worth and value for years. Now, she knew Jesus was no longer on that cross. The Lord had set her free. She'd prayed to God that if her story could help one person who'd also dealt with abuse, it would all be worth it. He took her pain and gave it purpose.

And now, it was like He was giving her yet another little gift in the form of that mystery man a couple of rows back.

Catt vowed to find out his name.

Stephen. It was Stephen, and he kept coming to her church. There were other men with him, but Catt couldn't recall their names, much less their faces. She prayed for Stephen by name for almost a year. She didn't know why, but she prayed. And prayed.

And prayed.

One day she showed up at a church event, and there he was. Her heart leaped in her chest. "Gosh," she thought. "I'm finally going to get to have that conversation, get to know what he's about."

Then, Catt noticed the girl with him. He was on a date!

But that was okay. It was fine. Because she knew he was going to be her husband. If anything, she felt a little bad for the girl.

You know what? she thought. *I'm going to pray for her because she doesn't know that she's out of here.*

About three months later they were married. Their faith and mission grew together. Now, they help others who have gone through abuse and addiction to find the incredible love of Jesus.

Piece It Together

Read 2 Samuel 12:18-25.

Even one of the greatest, most well-known men in the Bible experienced deep grief at the loss of a child. The Lord pulled him through.

What loss have you faced and how did the Lord pull you out of it? If you are still grieving, how do you feel the Lord comforting you?

_____

_____

_____

The people of the Bible were real with very real struggles. Whatever you're facing, you are not alone. Write a message to the Lord about your struggles; be real and honest with Him.

_____

_____

_____

Write your favorite Bible verse about God's comfort and then speak it out loud.

_____

_____

_____

Take a moment now to pray and ask God to comfort you as you face life's trials. Record anything He reveals to you during this time.

_____

_____

_____

GOD, YOU CAN HAVE HIM

"I'm pregnant." Christina's eyes were locked on the pregnancy test as a million different emotions slammed into her. Her stomach sank. This couldn't be happening. No.

She couldn't remember the last time she'd even talked to Josh. Now she was going to have to call him and tell him that he was the dad of the child now growing inside her? Yeah, she was definitely going to be sick.

She closed her eyes and rested her head against the wall. With a deep breath she sent Josh a text.

What happened next was a blur. There were tears. Discussions. Desperation, but one truth rang above them all: "Oh gosh, we need to fix this."

The next thing she knew, she was signing marriage papers. She blinked again, and she was holding her baby girl in her arms and suddenly she believed everything did happen for a reason, because she loved this girl with every beat of her heart.

This could work. Maybe this family could work. She could close her eyes and see Josh and herself raising this girl into someone better than themselves and she loved it.

But the dream shattered quickly, fracturing into a million pieces. Postpartum dragged her down. At first, Josh tried to hide his own struggles, but Christina knew. She could read the signs.

She had a newborn baby on one side of her and an addict on the other. Legal trouble and substance abuse were poisoning her family. It wasn't long before the divorce papers were in her hand. She'd tried. Surely, God and the world could see that she'd tried. She lifted the pen, ready to sign.

But she couldn't quite do it.

She cried out in a sob, "I've tried everything except surrendering. Josh is yours, God. You can have him 'cause I sure can't fix him."

Christina put the divorce papers away.

Some time later, her phone rang. She reluctantly took Josh's call, bracing for a fight.

"I think I want to go to True Purpose Ministries," he said.

Christina's breath caught. "Like, the place where they help people with addiction?" Christina asked, not quite daring to believe it.

"Yeah."

Christina watched as Josh gave up everything for ninety days: his possessions, his pride, his freedom. At the same time, she got her best friend back. Finally, she could recognize that man she'd dated, that man she'd fallen in love with.

Together, their world began to heal.

Piece It Together

Read Proverbs 3:5-6.

What do you have to surrender to God right now, trusting that He will make it right?

_____

_____

_____

_____

How can you surrender it and continue to surrender it day after day?

_____

_____

_____

_____

Write your favorite Bible verse about surrender and then speak it out loud.

_____

_____

_____

_____

Take a moment now to pray and ask the Lord to help you surrender everything to Him. Record anything He reveals to you during this time.

_____

_____

_____

_____

FREE FALLING

Terror filled Jayme as she stared down at the earth thousands of feet below. Underneath the bubbling fear was a boiling excitement. It was time to leave the plane, and something told her that she would love this.

She took a deep breath and jumped, wind whipping at her face. Her arms were outstretched as the world zipped by. *This is what freedom feels like*, she thought. *This is what living feels like*.

Free falling 15,000 feet from an airplane felt like going a month without binging and purging herself. Bulimia had ruled her life. Her childhood perfectionism grew into a check-the-box relationship with God, food-restricting diets, and over-exercising. It ate away at her. Her relationship with her husband broke down. Finally, she left him and fled to Florida.

She started dating an atheist. One day they drove by a church and he said, "I know you used to go to church when you lived in Michigan, and if the only reason you're not going now is because you don't want to go by yourself, I'd go with you."

An atheist. Telling her to go to church. In that moment, she knew it had to be God, so she took a chance and tried church again. It didn't lead to recovery right away. She tried seeing a counselor, but she wasn't ready yet. The hold bulimia had over her was just too strong. The craving twisted her mind. If she didn't give in, she just knew she would die. And yet, to keep purging was killing her.

Something had to change. It was time to start trying to recover. She had nothing left to lose trying it God's way. She cried out even though she was terrified.

What if I gain weight?

What if all these bad things happen that I don't have control of?

Her thoughts spun wildly, but she had to let go of control and start getting help. She came across a book written by someone who had dealt with bulimia. She saw herself in the pages of the book, only this person had gotten better. The story was enough to make Jayme realize it was time to start taking tiny, gradual steps.

She went one day without purging.

A week.

At the one-month mark, she signed up for skydiving. She had struggled so long that she didn't know who she was anymore. She didn't have hobbies or dreams. She needed something new. How different could you get than launching yourself out of a plane and into the sky?

As soon as her feet touched the ground, she knew everything was different. That free fall was what it felt like to be free from bulimia and she'd never forget it. There was no going back. She started traveling the world—even bungee jumping in Switzerland—and she knew was traveling with Him. Just her and the Lord.

She's now gone eight years without purging. Jayme thought

she'd live with this addiction her entire life, but God had a different plan. She has even hosted a podcast, *Recover With God Podcast*, to encourage others struggling with eating disorders.

It was a long journey that led to jumping out of that plane, but she now lives every day in beautiful, God-given freedom.

Piece It Together

Read Psalm 139:13-18.

What does this passage say about who you are?

_____

_____

_____

_____

How does the way God sees you change the way you see yourself?

_____

_____

_____

_____

Write your favorite Bible verse about who God says you are and then speak it out loud.

_____

_____

_____

_____

Take a moment now to pray and ask the Lord to help you see yourself the way He sees you. Record anything He reveals to you during this time.

_____

_____

_____

_____

THERE IN THE GRASS

Blades of grass scratched against Eric's cheek. The liquor store was only a few strides away, but he couldn't move. The night wrapped around him as hopelessness weighed down his chest.

"I'm done," he murmured. He wanted it all to end. How could he make it all end? "God, either something has to change right now, or I'm done with everything." He had no clue if the prayer would be heard.

"Eric?" A voice called in the distance. "Oh, man. Eric!" Hands shook his shoulder and Eric groaned as he turned his head to blink up at the person who had found him.

It was his drug dealer. He took Eric to the hospital. Mere days later, Eric found himself at True Purpose Ministries. God had heard his hopeless prayer. Things did change. The discipleship program helped Eric dive deeper into who God was. The Lord wasn't the angry, vengeful God he'd grown up hearing about. No, this God was a God of love. He realized he was part of His family. It was like he had the very DNA of the creator of the world.

From the age of sixteen, Eric had wanted to live freely in the world, able to do whatever he wanted. God let him. But when Eric was finally ready for change, He was right there waiting.

Now, Eric works at True Purpose Ministries where he sees lives changed every single day. He went from living in addiction to helping guys get out of addiction. He's been clean for nineteen months and counting. His drug dealer has even gotten clean!

Eric begged God to bring about change, and He heard him there in the grass.

Piece It Together

Read 1 John 5:14-15.

What does it mean to you that the Lord hears our prayers?

_____

_____

_____

_____

Take a moment today to write about something you have struggled to talk to God about.

_____

_____

_____

_____

Write your favorite Bible verse about answered prayers and then speak it out loud.

_____

_____

_____

_____

Take a moment now to pray and ask the Lord to give you the confidence to boldly approach Him. Record anything He reveals to you during this time.

_____

_____

_____

_____

THE MAN CYCLE

Age two: Melinda's mom and dad divorced.

Age four: Melinda's mom remarried.

Age ten: Divorced again.

Age eleven: Remarried.

Age fifteen: Divorced.

A boyfriend followed that.

For as long as Melinda could remember, she'd watched her mother cycle through men. It created chaos, and there were no constants in her life. She moved thirty-eight times and went to eight different schools. No one ever stayed. When men left her mom, they left her, too. If her life wasn't in turmoil, everything felt strange and wrong.

So, as an adult, she started her own cycle:

Age eighteen: Moved in with her boyfriend.

Not long after, she moved in with her first husband.

Divorced.

Lived with her second husband. That turned abusive. She left him.

For the first time, she was living on her own as a single mom. It was so much easier to focus on taking care of her kids and getting to know this God person without the toxic relationships seeping out in her life. Jesus was her Band-Aid. If she was bleeding, she kept Him close, only to rip Him off the moment she felt she no longer needed Him.

She got a new boyfriend and moved in with him. She was pregnant when the world spun crazy again, but something was different. For the first time, she didn't like the chaos.

She and her boyfriend split up and something in Melinda broke. She couldn't keep doing this. She didn't want to live like this anymore. She thought she'd had control of things but was barely scraping by. Truth was, *nothing* was inside her control.

"God, if You are real, save me."

An almost audible voice answered, "When will you stop putting other men before Me?"

Melinda sucked in a deep breath. "Right now."

She was always so quick to grab the next person when someone left her. She didn't want to do that again. No, whether her boyfriend came back or not, she just wanted Jesus.

She started Googling where to start with this whole Christian thing. Online pastors helped guide her through the Bible and she read prolifically. It opened her eyes. She'd spent her whole life just opening the door a crack to chat with Jesus. This time she was like, "Get in here!"

Melinda and her daughter were baptized together by a river. Afterward, she walked up to the bathhouse and looked at herself in the mirror. She studied her brown curls and dark eyes behind her glasses. She looked over every pore in her skin. She'd seen herself a thousand times, but it was like seeing a beautiful brand-new face. In that moment, she could see herself how the Lord saw her. Tears welled up in her eyes and poured down her cheeks. She was loved as she was. Nothing she could do or had done would change that. Jesus loved her and that was enough.

Her boyfriend did come back and they were married. A few months later, he got saved as well. Melinda gradually got used to the man in her life praying over her. She learned to trust him as he grew with the Lord, too. She'd never seen the marriage she has now. Once, love was a fleeting feeling. Now, it's on purpose. It is patient, kind, and loyal.

The cycle has broken.

Piece It Together

Read 1 Corinthians 13:4-8.

Do you love others like this passage describes? Give some examples.

_____

_____

_____

_____

Are there any cycles in your life you want—or need—to break?

_____

_____

_____

_____

Write your favorite Bible verse about love and then speak it out loud.

_____

_____

_____

_____

Take a moment now to pray and ask the Lord to help you love others the way He loves you. Record anything He reveals to you during this time.

_____

_____

_____

_____

THE CHEAT CODE

Kelton has the cheat code. Not to a video game or computer program. No, Kelton knows the secret to living a good, fulfilling life. It wasn't made up of digits or dashes but of a single name: Jesus.

But it took Kelton a while to figure that out. He had been in and out of church since he could walk. He had fantastic grandparents who loved the Lord. He was surrounded by faith but never really bought in. Seven years ago, he got into this cycle of focusing on himself and not others, definitely not on the Lord. He ignored the fact that he was Christian and filled his life with synthetic happiness: drugs, alcohol, strip clubs, and trap houses. He was only happy when he was doing the things he shouldn't, but that happiness never lasted long.

Kelton was present with his children but absent with his girlfriend. He was full of insecurities, depression, and anxiety. It wasn't long before he found himself incarcerated.

This isn't working, he thought. He was so tired of sleeping on a steel bunk. He was done hearing the lady say, "You have two minutes" when he was talking with his daughters. He decided to go to the judge with a plea to leave prison. Part of that deal was going to True Purpose Ministries. For a time, it seemed impossible. Kelton had to navigate grant deadlines and court dates, but finally, he was walking through the doors of this faith-based program with an open mind.

Within two weeks, things started changing for Kelton. Then came the moment that transformed everything. During worship, he looked over and noticed a girl nearly the same age as his daughter on her knees praising the Lord with hands pressed against the ground.

Kelton left the service and went to the back porch. He looked up at God. "I hear You. I'm answering the call."

That was the moment he fully gave his life to Jesus, and suddenly everything was new. He wasn't that alcoholic drug dealer anymore. He wasn't that depressed, anxious man anymore. He was no longer hopeless. No, he was brand new.

His relationship with his entire family began to heal. He saw his girlfriend—really saw her—for the first time in seven years. How many times had her eyes been telling him something he hadn't been willing to hear? No longer would he miss it. He never wanted to give her anything less than his undivided attention again.

He hugged his little girl and was truly in the moment. This was happiness. True, lasting happiness. What he experienced before was fake but this was real. No drug, no amount of money, no diamond chain could replicate this. Nothing had ever made him feel like this. Kelton heard of Jesus giving blind men back their sight, and he realized he had been blind. Not physically, but until he met Jesus he never saw the blessings that surrounded him.

There were still things that didn't make sense, but honestly, who cared? Who cared if it didn't all make sense if it changed his life for the better?

Kelton used to think Christianity was boring. Now, he jams to worshipful rap. He's living in the moment. Christianity can be cool. In just seven weeks, Kelton's life did a complete one-eighty, all because of Jesus. That's more than awesome.

Piece It Together

Read Isaiah 43.

Look closely at verses 18-19.

How did Jesus make everything new for you?

_____

_____

_____

_____

How is following Jesus fun and exciting for you?

_____

_____

_____

_____

Write your favorite Bible verse about a new life and then speak it out loud.

_____

_____

_____

Take a moment now to pray and thank the Lord for all the new things He's doing in your life. Record anything He reveals to you during this time.

_____

_____

_____

_____

TATTOOS

Problematic is tattooed across Joshua's forehead. He was called that as a child. *Heathen* is inked above his right eyebrow because he believed he was unworthy of forgiveness. Under his eye are the letters KYS, "kill yourself," because of the people who told him to end it all.

Those are just the tattoos on his face. Ink marks his neck, hands, and arms. He had needles stain lies under his skin, but God told him all of that was untrue. Now, those tattoos are a testament to how far he's come.

Joshua's childhood was turbulent. His abusive father went to prison after nearly beating his mom to death. Joshua burned down his family house at just two years old and was yanked from his mother's arms. He spent three years in a psychiatric and behavioral hospital where he was diagnosed with ADHD. They put him on a daily medication, which became the start of his stimulant addiction. By age eleven, he was self-medicating. It wasn't long before he'd been a prisoner in several different states and seven different prison facilities.

Then came the breaking point.

Joshua's twenty-five-year-old autistic niece became sick with Covid. Before she slipped into a coma and passed away, she said, "Tell my Uncle Josh that I love him. I never gave up on him, and I wish he'd get his life right."

She held such a big piece of Joshua's heart.

Of his life.

And now she was gone.

Who was he to be in prison instead of with his family? What if it had been his kids who had passed away while he was behind bars?

I'm as bad as my father, he thought.

But Joshua wanted better.

He hit his knees. "Guide me. I'm done with this life. I need You to show me how to change. Show me how I can be a better man and live a loving life. I want to spread love to people that need it."

Joshua spent the next sixteen months in his cell reading his Bible or crying. There was so much trauma and pain to work through. He had to slug through giant pools of dark memories. It was like struggling through tar.

Or ink.

He got off the bus from prison and entered True Purpose Ministries. He didn't talk much, coming off standoffish and rude as grown men told him they loved him.

It was weird at first, no doubt, but also a nice change. People weren't just saying the words, "I love you." They were showing him how to live it out day by day.

Now, he has graduated from True Purpose Ministries and is in college full-time. He volunteers to mentor incarcerated and other troubled youth. This man who hardly spoke when he got out of prison is now speaking into children's lives. He went from silence to being an influence.

And he tells those kids his stories through his tattoos. "See this? I thought I was unloved. See this? I thought my life was hopeless. But guess what, there are people out there who care. You just got to find them."

It took Joshua thirty-eight years to find his worth in Christ, but no longer do his tattoos tell the story of his pain. They tell the story of triumph from his past.

"Now, I just want to love on people. Like that teddy bear you can draw on with a marker, I'm just a big ol' tatted teddy bear."

Piece It Together

Read Acts 9:1-19.

Saul, who is also called Paul, became the man who penned much of the New Testament. But notice in this Scripture, when the Lord came to him, he was still seeking to murder Christians.

What made Saul worthy of being used by God? Are you any different?

_____

_____

_____

What from your past can help you connect with others to share God's love?

_____

_____

_____

Write your favorite Bible verse about your worth in Christ and then speak it out loud.

_____

_____

_____

Take a moment now to pray and ask the Lord to use your pain for purpose. Record anything He reveals to you during this time.

_____

_____

_____

_____

THE WALK AWAY

Charlie tugged on her aunt's sleeve until she leaned closer. Charlie whispered into her ear, "Please help me get my mother away from him. Get her out of the situation she's in." Her words turned into a prayer, "Lord, please save my mom."

Her mom, Tara, had stayed away to hide the bruises on her face, trapped in the toxic relationship that put them there. Trapped from all the decisions in her past that had gotten her to this point. She'd grown up with a good family and a grandfather who always kept them in church but she'd developed a lying problem. It only got worse in her teen years. She would be whoever and do whatever was necessary to fit in.

Tara didn't know who she was. She felt so empty. She was never happy. She started smoking pot. Then it was pills. Next, alcohol. Meth came later when she started dating a guy who used it. She just gave herself away and cycled through one bad relationship after another. She looked for love in all the wrong places and was so, so lonely. A loud voice in her mind kept saying she'd never be loved, and then an actual human being backed that up.

"What's wrong with you?" Tara's dad asked one evening.

"You're barely calling your daughter."

Tara dropped her gaze. "I just think she's better off without me."

Her dad ran a hand down his face. "You think that you're better off without your mom?"

The words were a gut punch. Tara's mom had passed away and she missed her so much it hurt. "N-no. Of course not."

Tara's dad pointed at Charlie. "Go ask that six year old if she's better off without you."

Tara didn't answer. There was nothing she could say to that.

It took her a week, but at last she came around. She got accepted into True Purpose Ministries. But there was one glaring obstacle: the bad boyfriend.

"Lord, please," she pleaded. "Make a way for me to get away from him."

Only a few minutes later, her abuser stood up. "I'll be back right back."

Tara knew this was her chance. He never went away and here he was leaving.

So, Tara left, too. She walked away, calling her family for a ride. A few days later, she was in True Purpose Ministries and getting the help she needed.

It wasn't too late to start over. Now, not only has she gained custody of her daughter, but she also has a 4.0 GPA in her youth ministry degree program. She lost everything, but as soon as she gave all to God—as soon as she walked away from her old life—God was there to give her back everything immeasurably more and better.

The hardest part was that first step.

Piece It Together

Read Luke 15:11-32.

What do you need to walk away from to start moving towards home?

_____

_____

_____

_____

What steps can you take today?

_____

_____

_____

_____

Write your favorite Bible verse about coming back to Christ and then speak it out loud.

_____

_____

_____

_____

Take a moment now to pray and ask the Lord to help guide you home. Record anything He reveals to you during this time.

_____

_____

_____

_____

ARE YOU OKAY?

"Are you ready to order?" Gage asked.

The man looked up at Gage from over his menu. "Son, are you okay?"

The question made Gage freeze. "Er, yeah. Of course…"

The man gave his order but that piercing look didn't leave his eyes.

"I'll be back with your drink," Gage mumbled and made a bee-line through the maze of tables to the drink dispenser in the back. Something about that question dug under his skin. His hands gripped the counter in front of him.

Was he okay? He honestly hadn't thought about it. But now that he did…

When he was seventeen, he'd gotten his girlfriend pregnant. She moved to Columbus, Ohio, with her family and of course he followed. That was his child, after all.

Just a few years back, his good friend died from a fentanyl overdose. Now, Gage was constantly drinking. He'd gotten two DUIs within his first eight days after moving back home. Several hundred dollars were in his back pocket to pay his bail next time he was arrested. He'd run from cities and places but he couldn't seem to outrun himself.

His hands started shaking. I'm not okay. Maybe I'm not okay.

Gage shook his head. He was being stupid. That man didn't know him and had no place asking him something like that. Gage would just ignore it. He topped off the drink and went back to the man's table.

The man tilted his head. "Are you sure you're okay?"

Gage snapped, "Yes. I'm fine." He placed the drink down. "What's your deal? Please stop talking to me."

The man tilted his head. "Can you sit down and let me talk to you?"

Gage arched his eyebrows. "I'm working."

The man's gaze flicked around the restaurant. The empty, middle-of-the-day restaurant. "I think you have time."

Hesitantly, Gage slid into the chair across from him, and the man began to speak. He told stories about Jesus and his twenty-four international missions trips. He talked about his time in Africa. He asked about Gage's own life, and something shifted. Gage leaned in closer to hear what the man might have to say.

Finally, the man paid for his meal and left, but as Gage was circling the table one last time, he spotted a note left behind with Gage's name and a phone number.

The next day, Gage called him and once again they talked.

"Gage, would you join me at a prayer conference?" the man asked.

Gage had no reason to say no. He went with the man and

everything he heard was different. Hopeful. Life changing. He received the Lord and was born again. Suddenly, everything was new. The next several months were spent living completely free.

Then, he moved back north. It wasn't long before he was back around the wrong people. One night, he was at a bar shooting pool. As he lined up the cue stick, a guy asked, "Hey, you want something where you can drink all night and at the end of the night, if you take this drug, you won't be drunk anymore and you can drive home?"

A grin spread across Gage's face. "Well, yeah. That sounds like magic."

The guy handed Gage a small bag of white powder—cocaine—and that changed everything.

No longer was he going out to drink alcohol. No, he'd graduated from that. Now, he was going out to get high using cocaine. It cost him nearly $750 a week to finance his hobby. He added methamphetamines later.

His addiction stretched on for two years, but he wasn't ignorant. Warning bells went off in his head as he reached for the drugs, a sick feeling lingering in his gut. He knew what God had done for him way back at that prayer conference. He knew he'd been given a second chance, and he knew he was blowing it. But how could Gage go to God now after taking His blessing and throwing it away? The thought turned his stomach.

Something had to change. Finally, he called his parents and explained the problem. "We're headed your way," they said. They picked him up and dropped him off at True Purpose Ministries.

There was a letter waiting for him. Gage's mouth dropped.

He didn't even have the whole information packet yet. How had someone found his address?

He slid his fingernail into the letter to open it. He read the first line and his chest nearly exploded. How was this possible? He knew the sender. It was from the man from the restaurant.

Once he was pulled out of that dark cycle of drugs and bad influences, he started to see the light again. Started to remember God's love again and he returned to Him.

That was over six years ago. He met his wife in the program, got married, and started a family. He's now a dad, counselor, and True Purpose Ministries program director.

The man from the restaurant is still a mentor in Gage's life. They have even gone to Africa together. That man's simple act of obedience began the rest of Gage's story.

Gage definitely wasn't okay when the man first asked him that question, but, dear friend, he is more than okay now.

Piece It Together

Read 1 Corinthians 2:9.

I want you to sit for a moment and close your eyes. Imagine how your future could go. Now, imagine something better happening. What's even better than that? Write it down. The amazing thing is, what the Lord has in store is even greater than we can imagine.

_____

_____

_____

_____

_____

So, how do you start towards that path? Try this:

- Read God's Word.
- Pray often.

Do the opposite of what your sinful instincts tell you to do. Break the negative patterns you've set for yourself. Call those parents you've been avoiding. Give an honest answer to the man who dares to talk to you at the restaurant.

Be brave.

What habits do you need to change?

_____

_____

_____

_____

Write your favorite Bible verse about God's great plans for you and then speak it out loud.

_____

_____

_____

_____

_____

Take a moment now to pray and ask the Lord to help you change your bad habits. Record anything He reveals to you during this time.

_____

_____

_____

_____

_____

TOGETHER

Sabrina gripped the steering wheel as tears poured down her face. Her chest was tight and each breath was a struggle. She was just. So. Scared. Through that door were people who would see right through her. All of her defenses would be pulled down. Sure, the greeters at the door were smiling, but what if she really was just too broken? What if they rejected her? What if she couldn't fit in?

Questions and doubts whirled in her head even as she put the car in park and turned the key off. She sucked in a deep breath, opened up the door, and took one shaky step forward. Then another. And another.

That was the process of her first trip to Celebrate Recovery. Fear dug roots down deep and wouldn't be torn up so easily. It helped that her friend invited her that first time, sitting with her through the whole event, but the fear made it hard to breathe. But she still went. Because sometimes, that's what it takes: pulling into a parking lot and taking that step even when it is difficult.

While working through the steps of Celebrate Recovery, she peeled layers back from her life and laid down the pains of the past. She laid down her loneliness left over from childhood, and she laid down her trauma after being abused as a child. She began a journey towards sobriety. Celebrate Recovery talked about forgiveness and making amends. Sabrina went to her dying mother's side and gave her mom the chance to look her in the eye and say, "I'm so sorry, Baby."

Soon after, her brother's girlfriend passed away. Her brother's death quickly followed—both from drug overdoses. The pain of loss stabbed down to Sabrina's core, but it didn't destroy her.

For years, she'd isolated herself in alcoholism. Now, she had a family of fellow broken people. The people in her Celebrate Recovery chapter came around her, their love mirroring that of Jesus. They lifted her up and challenged her to grow. Her group of girls listened closely, prayed well, and came alongside her.

She's faced trial after trial, fear after fear, but now she doesn't have to face them alone.

Life is so much better when it's lived in community.

Together.

Piece It Together

Read Galatians 6:2.

We were never meant to go through life alone. If you're struggling, don't isolate yourself. Don't suffer alone. God created community for us; we just have to be brave enough to enter into it. Brainstorm some places where you can find a godly community.

_____

_____

_____

_____

Who in your life is struggling and how can you help carry their burdens?

_____

_____

_____

_____

Write your favorite Bible verse about friendship and then speak it out loud.

_____

_____

_____

_____

Take a moment now to pray and ask the Lord to give you opportunities to help others. Record anything He reveals to you during this time.

_____

_____

_____

_____

DEEPER

Anthony was born on the Cherokee reservation. He married his first wife at fifteen and had a daughter. Not long after, he started smoking pot and got divorced.

His troubles got deeper.

He married his second wife and started doing meth. That relationship also fell apart.

His drug use got deeper.

To support his habit, he started selling drugs. The more he used, the more he sold. The more he sold, the more he used. It all pulled him down deeper.

Deeper.

Deeper.

Deeper.

He caught some charges and started a prison cycle. He'd parole out, go to church, only to relapse and go right back behind bars. He was separated from his dad, his brother, and from the rest of his family.

Deeper and deeper he dug his own prison, his own grave. He

was trapped with no way out, stuck at the bottom of the well of hopelessness he'd made.

But God reached down and made a way.

In prison, Anthony rededicated his life to the Lord and was baptized. He met his new wife and now has a beautiful son.

Life got so much deeper.

Love was deeper. No longer did it mean the people you got high and partied with. Love was the steadfast, indescribable commitment to his wife and son. Family relationships got deeper. He no longer had to wait for a visit in jail but could talk to his father and brother whenever he wanted.

At only three months clean, Anthony is learning that with Jesus, life just keeps getting deeper.

Deeper.

And deeper.

Piece It Together

Read Psalm 146.

How does walking with the Lord make your life deeper and richer?

_____

_____

_____

_____

Why do you think the Lord is worthy of praise?

_____

_____

_____

_____

Write your favorite Bible verse about the depths of God's love and then speak it out loud.

_____

_____

_____

_____

Take a moment now to pray and thank God for the deeper things in your life. Record anything He reveals to you during this time.

_____

_____

_____

_____

_____

_____

JOY IN THE MORNING

"Dad! Dad, please." Jonathan struggled to reach his son. The scene changed. Now, he was looking at a shirt just as it busted open from a gunshot wound. He woke up, heart pounding and fighting back a scream.

The nightmares wouldn't leave Jonathan alone. It was his mind's way of torturing him with the truth: his son was gone.

All his son had been trying to do was give a friend a streaming service password, but someone else was at the house—someone who was high and paranoid. He shot the young man in the back as he was leaving.

First, came the shock. This couldn't be happening. Just a few weeks ago, Jonathan's son was getting baptized. He didn't miss church for six straight Sundays. He'd met a really sweet girl. Jonathan had spent so many afternoons working on cars with his boy. He couldn't be gone.

But he was. Poof. A whisp in the wind.

The shock gave way to anger, a burning fury that consumed Jonathan. He wanted to retaliate, to take matters into his own hands. But he knew those thoughts led nowhere good and instead reached for drugs to drown them out. The drugs kept his energy up while the nightmares stole his sleep. He forced himself to go to work to support the family he had left. He had to care for his wife.

Money started running low. There just wasn't enough paycheck to keep up with the drugs. The anger began to fizzle out, leaving a deep depression in its place. He wasn't going to take his life, but if someone took it from him... he wouldn't mind.

His parole officer was watching and waiting for the chance to step in. Four months later, Jonathan failed his urine analysis and stood before a judge. True Purpose Ministries was presented as an option, and he took it, not that he wanted to go. He wanted something short. Easy. *Just let me get back to my wife. Just let me get back to my life.*

He got to True Purpose and they surprised him. The people were smiling and loving. Their pupils were the right size, not dilated from drug use. They invited him to a get-together that first day, and he got to grill the hot dogs. On the van back to the houses, he stared out the window. "Man, I'm gonna try this," he murmured.

He laid down in bed for a few hours that night but then had to get up to go to the restroom. Something shifted in his head and his knees hit the tile floor. Tears streamed down his face.

"Lord, I want to do this. I want this opportunity."

Jonathan found a new excitement in the classes, scribbling down notes. When his wife visited him, he shared everything he was learning, his eyes shining. His excitement was contagious. His wife started taking notes at home, too, and they studied together.

His wife had been at her bedside praying for her husband. She'd cried out while driving, begging God for change. Now, she saw so much growth, so much light.

Together, Jonathan and his wife turned their focus 100 percent to Jesus. Through Him, they found it in their hearts to forgive the man who had shot Jonathan's son.

Jonathan had spent a long, long night in a dark place of grief, anger, and depression, but joy came in the morning.

Praise the Lord.

Piece It Together

Read Psalm 30:5.

How long has your "night" been?

_____

_____

_____

_____

No matter what trial you face, there is still good to be seen in this life. Write yourself an encouraging note reminding you that the time for rejoicing is coming.

_____

_____

_____

_____

Write your favorite Bible verse about joy and then speak it out loud.

_____

_____

_____

Take a moment now to pray and ask the Lord to help you find joy in the trials. Record anything He reveals to you during this time.

_____

_____

_____

_____

GOD, I WANT TO BE LOVED

"Go to church with me?" Jody's friend asked.

Jody scratched the back of his head. "Church isn't my thing, but sure, man. I'll do you a favor."

The friend's mouth twitched with a smile.

Sunday rolled around and Jody followed his friend into the small country church. He scanned the room. There couldn't have been more than twenty-five people there. Jody shifted his weight. It was probably too obvious to leave now, right? The last place he wanted to be was in this church.

They sang a couple of songs and then a guy got up and started spouting off this stuff about salvation. He'd been a drunk, a brawler, and a terrible friend. The words hit too close to home, and immediately it was like Jody's eyes were opened. He could see himself: his alcohol addiction, his relationship with his second wife after the first committed suicide by overdosing, and the son who barely knew him. He saw the turbulent childhood that led him to that pew, but there was nothing for Jody to do about it. He shook off the thoughts and started to leave.

"Hey," his friend stopped him. "The Lord's telling me that I need you to come back with me tonight."

Jody didn't get that whole "the Lord told me" thing, but he was leaving the next day anyway. It's not like he would have to stick around for any more of this church thing. "Sure."

That night, another man got up to speak about the struggles with alcohol in his life. He compared his story to a man named Saul in the Bible who had a radical encounter with the Lord.

Next thing Jody knew, his feet were taking him down the aisle straight to the altar. He thought he knew what he might say there on his knees but instead, all that came out was, "God, I want to be loved."

A hand pressed against his back, a friend praying over him. Something seemed to gush into Jody's body. New strength poured into his body. Jody didn't understand what happened but when he stood up and walked out of that church, he put down the vodka bottles. He stopped going through a case of beer a day. He just quit. Cold turkey.

There had been so much pain in Jody. He'd come back from combat in 2007, where he was in charge of forty-eight soldiers who all dealt with things in two ways: fists or the bottle. Just a few years after getting back, six of his soldiers committed suicide with overdoses. For years, he'd been a functioning alcoholic trying to make enough money to buy people's favor, to buy their love. It had left him with a giant void, but the Lord's love was moving in to fill all the empty space of pain.

"Dude, I got you," He seemed to say. "I will love you like nobody else. When everyone else stops loving you, I will love you more."

Jody turned his back on his six-figure career and took the job offer to work in vocational rehabilitation. He traded his boats, cars, and motorcycles for lasting happiness. God never wanted Jody's money. He wanted his time and his service. He wanted Jody to take his son to a ball game. He wanted Jody to take a day with his wife and help out at church. Now, Jody uses his story to speak into hopeless lives at halfway houses and rehabilitation services. He still has struggles and hard days—his own son is on a slow recovery journey—but through it all, he doesn't have that hole in his heart anymore.

"God, I just want to be loved," he asked.

And God answered.

Piece It Together

Read John 3:16.

Try to memorize this verse if you haven't already!

What worldly things have you done to try to gain people's love?

_____

_____

_____

_____

How does it make you feel that God loves you so much He sent His only Son to die for you?

_____

_____

_____

Write your favorite Bible verse about how much God loves you and then speak it out loud.

_____

_____

_____

_____

Take a moment now to pray and meditate on how deeply loved you are by your Father. Record anything He reveals to you during this time.

_____

_____

_____

_____

DEAD TO LIFE

Her eyes opened for the first time in months. Doctors asked her questions. People smiled at her like they knew her, but all of the faces blurred together.

My name… what is my name?

Her insides twisted. She didn't know anything. Not who she was. Not how to read or write or do simple math. They told her she was a sophomore in high school, but the past was just a black hole.

Gradually, the memories started to come back. Jocelyn. Her name was Jocelyn. She'd made more friends her freshman year. She'd been in a car accident. She could hear the argument between the driver and his girlfriend. "I'll just kill us all," he'd said as he went up the hill and flipped the car. She could see a burst of red and orange as the vehicle burst into flames.

Then, there was nothing. Jocelyn had died. For a few seconds, there was no beat in her heart and no breath in her lungs. They called in medevac and managed to bring her back to life in the helicopter, but she was comatose.

When she finally did wake up, she had to relearn everything. She went back to school the second semester of her sophomore year but was light years behind. Teachers took her back to elementary math to catch her up, but it was a struggle. Every day was a fight. She found solace in her music class. At least that was one passion not even death could kill.

Jocelyn eventually moved in with a friend, and there were accessible drugs in that house. She partied and rarely went to school the rest of high school. Only the No Child Left Behind Act pushed her through and she graduated.

She met a boy. He was older than her by quite a few years but that didn't matter. She loved him. Dearly. She'd have done anything in the world for him. She used her car accident payout to buy them a house. Dreams for the future blossomed in her mind but they were quickly crushed. He broke her heart.

Jocelyn started using more to block out the pain. There wasn't much of anything she cared about. She failed drug tests and constantly found trouble. Her next relationship ended in a domestic assault. At the hospital, they discovered she was pregnant.

She'd never thought she could get pregnant. She'd never wanted to get pregnant, and now a baby grew inside her. How was she going to raise a child when she couldn't even keep herself away from drugs?

"God, I don't really know You," she murmured, "but I really hope You can actually hear me, save me, and get me out of this life."

Jocelyn moved back to Tennessee, turned herself in because of a warrant, and ended up at True Purpose Ministries. Her daughter was born while she was in the program and she was able to stay with her the whole time.

One afternoon, she was sitting on the porch and a lady struck up a conversation. Jocelyn told her story and how everything had lined up to get her into this program. "I don't know how all of this happened in the perfect timing. It just all worked out perfectly."

The lady cocked her head. "It wasn't you, honey."

The words sank in deep. That was Jocelyn's first "but God" moment.

From there, her faith only grew. Her relationship with her family healed. She has now been sober for two years. She knows God is real. She's seen Him work. She may have only been physically dead in that car crash for a few seconds, but spiritually she'd been dead so much longer. She's not dead anymore. Jocelyn is alive in Christ today!

Piece It Together

Read Ephesians 2.

Read the full passage, starting with verse 1.

Do you feel like you are living dead with sin or alive with Christ? What makes you feel this way?

_____

_____

_____

_____

_____

Christ is the only road to true life. If you have not given your life to Christ, pray today to ask Jesus to save you (Go to Accept Jesus Today for more information). If you have accepted Jesus as your savior, write down some ways you could go deeper in that relationship.

_____

_____

_____

_____

_____

Write your favorite Bible verse about salvation and then speak it out loud.

_____

_____

_____

_____

Take a moment now to pray and thank the Lord for saving you. Record anything He reveals to you during this time.

_____

_____

_____

_____

_____

THE MUSICIAN

Stage lights flashed in Raffa's eyes. This was living the dream. He went from church to church across Brazil singing and selling his recordings. His family was made up of musicians, so it was only natural. His dad sang, his mom played piano, and his grandfather played guitar. Music was his world… until it was all ripped away.

At eighteen, his parents left everything behind and moved their family to the United States. He didn't speak the language, and every face outside his home was a stranger's. Everything he'd built with his music came crashing down.

Why would You do that, God? Why would You take everything away from me? I was doing Your work!

He'd gone to church as a child and learned the theology. He knew a lot about Jesus and the stories of the Bible, but that's where his Christianity stopped. He had a relationship with theology and a relationship with music. There was no relationship with Jesus.

He'd been drinking, partying, and clubbing since he was sixteen but it only grew worse when he got to the US. Back in Brazil, there was a balance. A little bit of church for every bit of partying. When he moved, he quit going to church and got hooked on cocaine. Raves were especially exhilarating.

Yet there was a hole in his heart he couldn't seem to fill. He sought to fill it at parties but walked away emptier than he came. On his way home, he played CDs in his car. The only ones he had in the visor were gospel and Christian music, and he cried all the way home as he listened.

He always went to the next party, though.

Thirty-five people he called friends crammed into an apartment. Suddenly, he started feeling strange. His heart rate slowed. His head grew heavy. Sweat clung to his forehead. Blood dribbled out his nose. He closed his eyes as the world tunneled.

"God, don't let me die," he begged and was gone.

He woke later to an empty apartment. No ambulance. No police. He'd overdosed and the ones he'd called his friends had just left.

Raffa looked around. "God, I don't know what to do anymore. I don't know who to talk to. I—I've been in church. It's always the same."

An almost audible voice answered, "There are some places you're going to meet Me, but you need to *meet* Me."

Then it hit him. That Jesus he'd learned about was real. Really real. He may not see Him, but that didn't make Him any less true.

Still, Raffa struggled. Five months after the overdose, the loneliness threatened to consume him and he went back to another party, but this time was different.

"God, I'm not gonna lie. If someone asks if I want some drugs, I'm gonna take them. But… will You go with me?" Raffa prayed.

Sure enough, when he got to the party a guy asked, "Want to go into the Special Room?"

Raffa followed him. People sat around a table with white lines on it. Cocaine was waiting for him. Raffa just stared.

God is with me.

And those drugs are not what I want anymore.

That cocaine wasn't going to do Raffa any good. Drugs like that only led to heartache.

"You know what, man? I think I made a mistake." Raffa turned and left the room, leaving the drugs behind.

Life hasn't been easy since then. He had to battle cancer for a year, but through it all he had Jesus, a deep relationship with Jesus.

When Raffa toured in Brazil, he did it for the spotlight, for the music, and excused it as the Lord's work. Now, he truly does His work. Raffa is a worship leader, teacher, and music producer. He even has his own studio.

It was never about the work but about the relationship.

Piece It Together

Read Deuteronomy 31:6.

Invite Jesus to go with you. Everywhere with you. If there's a sin you're struggling with, dare to invite Him into the situation. It will always be better to go with Jesus than go alone. It's okay if you feel ashamed or afraid. Just ask Him to join you. He will never let you down, and I promise He will only make things better, even if it takes a little growing pain. Write Him a note, asking Him to be with you always.

_____

_____

_____

_____

_____

What talents do you have that the Lord wants you to surrender to Him?

_____

_____

_____

_____

Write your favorite Bible verse about how God is always with you and then speak it out loud.

_____

_____

_____

_____

_____

Take a moment now to pray and ask the Lord to show Himself to you no matter where you are. Record anything He reveals to you during this time.

_____

_____

_____

_____

_____

ABUNDANTLY MORE

No.

No, this couldn't be happening.

It just couldn't.

Ashley's boyfriend couldn't be dead. She was only sixteen, and he was only seventeen. The news that her first love was gone crushed her. Her lungs struggled to suck in air.

Her parents wanted her to keep smiling as if it was all okay, but Ashley couldn't do that. Nothing was okay. The pain wasn't something she could push down. She snuck out to go to the visitation and funeral. She wasn't better off without him, like they said.

The grief was agony. All she wanted was to see his smile again. To speak with him again. To feel his arm around her again. She'd do anything to dull the pain for just a moment, and that led her to start using. First, it was pot and drinking but a college boy introduced her to cocaine and that was that. Ashley was addicted to drugs.

For twenty years, that was her life. She tried seven rehabs and three detox programs. Her son and first daughter were taken from her. Her second daughter was taken away at the hospital after drugs were detected in them both. Ashley fought for her daughter but the foster parents won; she just wasn't stable enough.

There was rock bottom after rock bottom. She was homeless and strung out. She kept pictures of her kids and pieces of their clothing. She would look at them and cry for days in her car.

Eventually, she got pregnant again, but at twelve weeks she miscarried. She held his still body in her hands and looked into his tiny face. His eyes would never open. His lungs would never breathe air. The drugs Ashley used did this to him.

I can't keep living like this.

When she got home, she dug out her Bible and a Jesus Calling devotional. She sat in her room and cried as she read those books. For days she read and read.

As a little girl, all she wanted was to be a mother and a wife. How had life gotten so twisted up? She had the children she'd dreamed of, but drugs had kept her from being present with them. She'd had boyfriends but nothing was permanent. She wanted to be a stylist and cut hair but didn't even have a license to drive to work.

When she gave birth the next time, she vowed things would be different. She stared down into her new daughter's face. "God, this is it. Tell me what You want me to do. I want to live for You. I want to live for my kids."

"Call your parents," an almost audible voice answered back.

She reached for her phone. "Will you come pick my daughter and me up from the hospital?"

Her first year of recovery took place at her parents' house.

Covid was a blessing. It kept her at home where she could focus on putting her life back together, enjoying time with her newborn, and working on the relationship with her son. She found a church. She started working at Great Clips, her dad driving her there and back until she got her own driver's license. Thanks to a conversation with a hair client, she even got her own little apartment.

Everything looked so good until five days before Christmas when Great Clips fired her. She called her mom and cried. How was she going to pay for her kids' Christmas? How was she going to keep her apartment?

Her phone beeped with an incoming call.

"Mom, let me take this," Ashley said and accepted the call.

A woman from church answered, "You know when we talked about you going to a full-service salon?"

"Yes…" Ashley's heart skipped a beat.

"Well, I just got off the phone with the owner of one and she's looking for a stylist."

Tears of joy replaced the tears of sorrow.

Ashley dreamed of being a stylist. She could now work at a Christian-owned, full-service salon.

Ashley dreamed of being a mother. She now has custody of two of her four kids, with faith that she will one day reunite with her other two.

Ashley never thought she could dig herself out of the hole of addiction. She's now been clean for over five years. All because of Jesus.

The Lord will do exceedingly and abundantly more than we can ever imagine. The dreams you dreamed are there for a reason.

Piece It Together

Read Psalm 37:4.

When you read this verse, at first it may sound like the Lord will give you whatever you want, but there's a better way to understand this verse: the Lord gives you the desires you have. He places those desires in your heart. The desire to be loved is from Him. The desire to be a good parent is from Him. What are the deepest desires in your heart that may be straight from the Lord?

_____

_____

_____

_____

_____

What are the hopes and dreams you had as a child before life got in the way?

_____

_____

_____

_____

_____

Write your favorite Bible verse about hope and then speak it out loud.

_____

_____

_____

_____

_____

Take a moment now to pray and ask the Lord to show you the path forward to "exceedingly and abundantly." Record anything He reveals to you during this time.

_____

_____

_____

_____

_____

TABLETS

Mitchell may have never read the book as a free man, but in jail, the story sucked him in. He read about another man who had a drug addiction that had gotten him sentenced. Mitchell saw himself among the pages, but the author turned his life around. Mitchell still had a long way to go.

Mitchell wanted that. *Needed* that. He scrambled to grab a piece of paper and started writing out a contract to God. He poured his heart onto the page.

God the Father, Jesus the Son, and Holy Spirit, I give You my life to use as a tool for Your purpose.

There was a slight burning sensation deep inside Mitchell. He didn't know what it was, but it felt good.

He realized he needed to pray. "God, what am I supposed to do? What is the next step?" He asked the air, "How am I supposed to know You're with me?"

It was like a movie went off in his head. He watched all the things he'd done: the drug use, the gang violence, the cycle of girlfriends. Regret and remorse twisted in his gut.

"Repent," echoed through his head and heart.

Mitchell listened and repented to each thing as it was brought in front of his eyes.

That warm feeling from earlier burst into a full-out flame. He wanted God to move in his life. He was praying, talking to God, and reading His Word.

At the end of a three-day fast, a lady came to interview him for a rehab program. He left the interview feeling everything had gone well, but it wasn't meant to be. His application was denied due to his violent past, but he had still completed the jail time. He was released and stayed sober for about a month and a half. He read the Word daily and told others about God.

His dad invited him to come to his place, and Mitchell took him up on the offer. But it wasn't long before the long nights staying up late to work with his dad led him back to cocaine. One night, they clashed. His dad stabbed him with his own knife. Pain exploded in his gut.

There wasn't a home with his father anymore.

He lived in a market parking lot for six months. He was in and out of vans and cars. A fence off to the side of the parking lot made for a good place to build a little house. He was at the end of himself again, the contract with God a distant memory. He fell back into his old bad habits.

One night he was out wandering the streets eating some Xanax. He passed a mailbox and in his mind's hazy state, it suddenly seemed like a great idea to look inside. He started picking through the mail. Someone must have noticed him because the law came down on him. They searched everything on him and found a DUI from the past. They took him to jail.

It wasn't a book that caught his eye this time; his hands found Rio Revolution Church on a tablet. At first he watched because it was the only free thing on the tablet. He didn't know much about the church, but there was this tug in his chest as he watched. He was drawn to it.

Finally, he finished serving his time. It was late, at least 10:30 at night. Mitchell knew he had nowhere good to go.

"Can I stay another night?"

"No," the lady said, but found him a pillow and blanket so he could stay in the visitation room.

The next morning, he left and headed over to the probation office. "How much do I have left?"

"No, you're a free man. You can do what you want."

"Where's that church?" Mitchell asked.

They gave him directions and Mitchell started on his way. It started to rain. For a moment, he wanted to stop and rest, but something—the Holy Spirit—kept kicking him onward.

He was greeted at the church and they helped him come up with a plan. At first, True Purpose Ministries was full, so they started praying.

The phone pinged with a text: *We'll put you in a closet some-where.*

That was over three years ago. Now, Mitchell is a firm believer and son of God. Every morning, he suits up with the armor of the Lord. He studies and uses God's Word. He still faces difficult days but knows where to take it.

His testimony is now shared on the same tablets that led him back to church.

Piece It Together

Read Ephesians 6:10-18.

Describe your first encounter with Jesus and how it made you feel.

_____

_____

_____

_____

What does it mean to put on the armor of God and what would that look like on a daily basis?

_____

_____

_____

_____

Write your favorite Bible verse about encountering Jesus and then speak it out loud.

_____

_____

_____

_____

Take a moment now to pray and ask the Lord for an encounter with Him today. Record anything He reveals to you during this time.

_____

_____

_____

_____

DANIEL'S TESTIMONY

One more story left.

I want to introduce you to Daniel. He came into the interview for our YouTube series with nervous energy as if this was one of the first times he'd told his story. He wore a simple gray sweatsuit, a black T-shirt, and dark Hey Dudes. Tattoos peeked out from his sleeve and hoodie. An orange lanyard hung from his neck. He had a full beard and the biggest smile on his face.

The world may have looked at him and seen a recovering addict, but I looked at him and only saw a child of God. In his huge smile, I could feel how much the Lord loved the man sitting across from me.

"Tell me a little about yourself," I said.

His grin widened. "My name's Daniel. I'm a believer in Jesus Christ." His identity firmly rested not on *who* he was but *whose* he was.

He continued to tell his story. He'd struggled with substance abuse for over two years. He'd had a business and a house but lost it all due to his addiction. It started as recreational then passed that into the functioning addict zone until he was a full-blown addict. It tore at his relationship with his family. He stopped communicating with his wife, his kids, and the rest of those who loved him. He was chasing drugs into a place of darkness and wilderness, feeling utterly lost.

Finally, handcuffs clicked around his wrists at thirty-six years old. "You're going to jail, son," they said.

Reality crashed in around Daniel. *Dang, man. This was happening.*

But a prison cell was the best thing for him because he was forced to be still and dry out. There was a Bible in there with him, and he started to read it. Gradually, it was like the smoke cleared and he could see again.

When he was called in front of the judge, he begged, "If you're gonna let me out of here, take me to True Purpose Ministries."

Daniel had been wanting to go for a while but kept running from it. The drugs were just too enticing. But at True Purpose Ministries, he went clean for a full year. The people poured love into him. He made so much progress but did relapse and had to return for a few months.

In his own words, "I'm not where I want to be, but I'm in a really good place." Even once you start down the path of recovery, the road isn't always easy. Sometimes, it's a battle you face for the rest of your life. But with Christ, your story is different. If you try to recover on your own, you are at the whims of your own willpower, and willpower will fail. With Christ, you have the King of kings on your side.

Today, Daniel has peace and is loyally loved. He has started down the path of reconciling with his family. He's hit the reset button. Everything in the past is wiped out. It's time for a redo. You can come to this place, too. Your husband can. Your wife can. Your son can. Your daughter can. Your friend can.

It takes a conscious decision to pursue the Lord instead of the world. It takes work. It won't be easy. You'll have to forgive yourself, which may be the hardest type of forgiveness of all. You have to lay it all on the altar. You have to let the past burn up until there's nothing but smoke. You can't keep picking it back up.

Leave it.

Let it go.

And, dear friend, you'll discover your story is amazing. The Lord hasn't left you. He never left you. All the broken pieces are going to come together into a work of art.

And it will be beautiful.

Piece It Together

Read Revelation 12:11.

The Lord gives us our testimonies to use for His kingdom. What is yours?

_____

_____

_____

_____

_____

_____

_____

_____

_____

_____

_____

_____

_____

_____

_____

_____

_____

_____

_____

_____

_____

ACCEPT JESUS TODAY

Now is the best time to accept Jesus Christ as your Lord and Savior. If you declare with your mouth, "Jesus is Lord," and believe in your heart God raised Him from the dead, you will be saved (Romans 10:9).

Please consider believing this truth and saying these simple words: *Heavenly Father, I believe with my heart and confess with my mouth that Jesus rose from the dead so that I can be saved. I ask You to come into my life and forgive me of my sin. I want to live to bring glory and honor to You.*

Thank You, Lord.

Amen.

If you just prayed that prayer, I am so excited for you! You are not who you used to be. You have been made new! Please reach out to me if you have made this life-changing decision. I want to celebrate with you! Also, if you have additional questions about God's incredible Word, I would love to help you.

WHAT IS TRUE PURPOSE?

Many of these testimonies came from people who have gone through True Purpose Ministries. This fantastic organization helps men and women lead lives of lasting sobriety in order to fulfill their God-given purposes. They are located in Maryville, Tennessee, and have men and women sober living houses, as well as a pregnant women's home and couples' sober living home. True Purpose Ministries is committed to putting spiritual truth in the process of recovery.

If you or someone you know would like more information about True Purpose, you can visit www.truepurposeministries.com, email **tpmact@gmail.com**, or call (865) 681-4861.

WHAT IS CELEBRATE RECOVERY?

Celebrate Recovery is a grace-filled and biblically based community for anyone struggling. This community works together to bravely face pain and overcome it. The goal is simple: have a recovery that lasts. If you are interested in more information about this program, visit https://celebraterecovery.com/. There, you will be able to find local meetings and start connecting with other people on a journey towards healing.

WATCH THE FULL INTERVIEWS

Want more details about these incredible testimonies? You can watch the full interviews on YouTube at Katie Hauck Ministries, You Are Loved.

OTHER KATIE HAUCK MINISTRIES RESOURCES

COMING TO LIFE:

This is a comprehensive guide to the entire Bible. I'll walk you through each book and show you how it fits into God's big story. A workbook is available for purchase to help you on this Bible study journey. You can access the videos on YouTube or visit my website for more information.

ARE YOU A MARY OR A MARTHA?

Ladies, this one's for you. Most of us relate to one of these famous women of the Bible. Jesus tells Mary that she chose the better thing when she listened at the feet of Jesus instead of rushing around working, but does He love Mary more? The answer will surprise you.

USE YOUR KEYS

You've come to know Jesus. You have experienced life-changing, redeeming, and freeing power first hand. But while we are going to spend forever in Heaven, there are people we walk by every single day who do not know Jesus. Every day they're slowly dying on their way to Hell. Learn how to "use your keys" and unlock the gates caging them here before it's too late.

KATIEHAUCKMINISTRIES.COM

All of these materials can be found on my website, along with many more. If you want updates on future projects, join my newsletter. Also, don't forget to subscribe to my YouTube channel to continue hearing inspiring stories that will help you grow closer to Jesus.

ACKNOWLEDGMENTS

On behalf of the whole Katie Hauck Ministries team, thank you for reading *From These Broken Pieces.* If you purchased this book, you made it possible for another copy to find its way into recovery centers and prisons. If you found this book in your brokenness, we pray that it has helped you pick up your Bible and start piecing your life back together. We are praying for you and cheering for you! Please contact us if there is any way we can help.

I want to say thank you first and foremost to my amazing husband and family. You are always the support I need.

Thank you also to my church family, Rio Revolution Church, and all of my friends at Rio Revolution Celebrate Recovery.

Thank you, True Purpose Ministries, for opening up your doors so we could find these amazing people, and a million big thank yous to all the brave souls who shared their stories. The Lord is using you in mighty ways, and it was a joy to be a small part of that!

To my awesome ministry team: thank you, Laken Kimsey, for being the face behind the camera capturing all of these amazing stories. We couldn't have done this without you. Thank you,

Sharon Williams, Kathy Taylor, Amy Foss, and Ani Witt. You are all amazing! Also, a special thanks to Natalie Williams who first had the idea of turning the interviews into a book. You put so much heart into making it happen!

Most important of all, thank You, Jesus. You are the reason these stories exist. Only You can make broken things beautiful.

ABOUT KATIE HAUCK MINISTRIES

Katie is a business owner, orphan advocate, homeschool teacher, and ordained minister on top of being a wife and mother of eleven. Katie is the founder of Katie Hauck Ministries, which is designed to help believers ignite a passion for studying the Word of God in order to develop a more intimate relationship with Jesus. She and her team desire for you to know you are loved, for you to love others, and for you to read your Bible. Katie is living proof that God can take the broken and make it beautiful!

*"And we know that in all things God works
for the good of those who love Him, who have
been called according to His purpose."*

Romans 8:28

Notes